The All About Series

All About ...

DISCARDED

S0-BRU-962

Famous Canadians from Nova Scotia

Barb McDermott and Gail McKeown
Reidmore Books

Public Library
Incorporated 1862
Barrie, Ontario

Reidmore Books Inc.

18228 - 102 Avenue
Edmonton, AB T5S 1S7
phone (780) 444-0912
toll-free 1-800-661-2859
fax (780) 444-0933

website: http://www.reidmore.com
email: reidmore@compusmart.ab.ca

printed and bound in Canada

We acknowledge the financial support of the
Government of Canada through the
Book Publishing Industry Development Program (BPIDP)
for our publishing activities.

Canadä

©1999 Reidmore Books

All rights reserved. No part of this work covered by the copyrights hereon may be
reproduced or used in any form or by any means – graphic, electronic or
mechanical – without the prior written permission of the publisher. Any request for
photocopying, recording or information storage and retrieval systems of any part of
this book shall be directed in writing to the Canadian Copyright Licensing Agency,
6 Adelaide Street East, Suite 900, Toronto, ON M5C 1H6.

Canadian Cataloguing in Publication Data
McDermott, Barb.
All about famous Canadians from Nova Scotia

(All about series)
Includes index.
ISBN 1-896132-74-X

1. Nova Scotia--Biography--Juvenile literature. I. McKeown, Gail.
II. Title. III. Series: McDermott, Barb. All about series.
FC2305.M32 1999 j920.0716   C99-910760-7   F1036.8.M32 1999

About the Authors

Barb McDermott and Gail McKeown are highly experienced
kindergarten teachers living in Ontario. Both hold Bachelor of Arts and
Bachelor of Education degrees, Early Childhood diplomas, specialist
certificates in Primary Education, and have completed qualification
courses in Special Education. As well, Gail has a specialist certificate in
Reading and Visual Arts, and Barb has one in Guidance.

Credits

Editorial: Leah-Ann Lymer, Scott Woodley, David Strand,
Debbie Culbertson
Illustration, design and layout: Bruno Enderlin, Leslieanna Blackner Au
Maps: Wendy Johnson, Johnson Cartographics

Photo Credits

Cover and stamp photo: Sarah McLachlan, by Nettwerk
Page
3 Nettwerk/Crystal Heald
5 Nettwerk
7 Public Archives of Nova Scotia
9 Scott Woodley
11 Michael Bedford Photography
13 Flora MacDonald
15 Public Archives of Nova Scotia
17 Glenbow-Alberta Institute/NA-2473-1
19 Public Archives of Nova Scotia
21 Scott Woodley
23 Lupins Productions
25 Mark Mainguy/Lupins Productions
27 Sylvain Majeau

We have made every effort to identify and credit the sources of
all photographs, illustrations, and information used in this textbook.
Reidmore Books appreciates any further information or corrections;
acknowledgment will be given in subsequent editions.

Table of Contents

(All about what's in the book)

Introduction
(All about the beginning)

People who make the world a better place to live can become famous.

Canada has famous musicians, **inventors**, **politicians**, and sailors.

Many famous Canadians are from the **province** of Nova Scotia.

Sarah McLachlan (1968-)
(All about a famous Canadian musician)

Sarah McLachlan was born in Halifax.

She is a singer and song writer.

Her albums include *Surfacing*, *Solace*, and *Fumbling Towards Ecstasy*.

She has sold 1 000 000s of albums.

She has won many awards for her music.

Sarah McLachlan

Sarah McLachlan (1968-)
(All about a famous Canadian musician)

Sarah McLachlan sang at her 1st concert when she was 17 years old.

A person from a record company saw her sing at this concert and wanted her to make an album.

She waited 2 years before she decided to make an album for the company.

She started a music festival called Lilith Fair in 1996.

Lilith Fair celebrates musicians who are women.

Sarah McLachlan
Started Lilith Fair

Abraham Gesner (1797-1864)
(All about a famous Canadian inventor)

Abraham Gesner was born in Cornwallis.

He invented kerosene.

Kerosene is a **fuel** that gives a bright, white light when it is burne

Abraham Gesner was interested in rocks.

He worked as a **geologist** for the province of New Brunswick from 1838 to 1842.

Abraham Gesner

Abraham Gesner (1797-1864)
(All about a famous Canadian inventor)

Abraham Gesner was a medical doctor.

He had to ride his horse to sick people's houses to take care of them.

He would stop to collect rocks when he was travelling from 1 sick person's house to another.

He collected rocks from all over New Brunswick and Nova Scotia on his horse and in his canoe.

He opened Canada's 1st museum about rocks in 1842.

A Lamp Lit by Kerosene

Flora MacDonald (1926-)
(All about a famous Canadian politician)

Flora MacDonald was born in North Sydney.

She has been a politician and a television host.

She was the 1st woman to try to become leader of the Progressive Conservative **political party.**

She was the 1st woman to be the **minister of foreign affairs** in Canada.

She has won many awards for her work, including the Order of Canada.

Flora MacDonald

Flora MacDonald (1926-)
(All about a famous Canadian politician)

Flora MacDonald was **elected** to Canada's government in 1972.

She became the host of the television show "North/South" after she left Canada's government.

She travelled around the world to learn about people who live in countries where there is war or hunger.

She works with many groups that try to help these people, including CARE Canada and Mines Action Canada.

Royal Canadian Mint — Monnaie royale canadienne

Flora MacDonald Is a Politician

13

John Thompson (1845-1894)
(All about a famous Canadian politician)

John Thompson was born in Halifax.

He was the 4th **prime minister** of Canada.

He was **premier** of Nova Scotia and a **justice** in the Supreme Court of Nova Scotia before he became prime minister.

He helped to start Dalhousie Law School.

He believed that women should be allowed to vote.

John Thompson

John Thompson (1845-1894)
(All about a famous Canadian politician)

John Thompson became a lawyer when he was 20 years old.

He helped to create the Criminal Code of 1892.

The Criminal Code shows what is against the law in Canada.

John Thompson became prime minister in 1892.

He was prime minister for 2 years.

John Thompson Believed Women Should Vote

William Hall (1832-1904)

(All about a famous Canadian sailor)

William Hall was born near Summerville.

He was 1 of the 1st Canadians to win the Victoria Cross.

He was the 1st Canadian sailor and the 1st Black Canadian to win the Victoria Cross.

The Victoria Cross is an award for bravery.

He also won other medals for bravery.

William Hall

William Hall (1832-1904)

(All about a famous Canadian sailor)

William Hall started working on ships when he was about 12 years old.

He joined the British **navy** when he was 20 years old.

William Hall and the other sailors on his ship had to join a battle in India.

William Hall won the Victoria Cross because he kept firing his cannon until the enemy ran away.

He bought a farm in Canada after leaving the navy.

The Victoria Cross

Rita MacNeil (1944-)
(All about a famous Canadian musician)

Rita MacNeil was born in Big Pond.

She is a singer and song writer.

Her albums include Home I'll Be and Music of a Thousand Nights.

She had her own television show called "Rita and Friends."

She has won many awards, including the Order of Canada and Juno Awards.

Rita MacNeil

Rita MacNeil (1944-)
(All about a famous Canadian musician)

Rita MacNeil moved to Toronto when she was 17 years old.

She worked to become a famous singer in Toronto.

She became famous when she sang at a fair in Vancouver in 1986.

She has sold 1 000 000s of albums.

She owns a popular restaurant in Nova Scotia.

Rita MacNeil Is a Famous Singer

Summary
(All about the ending)

Canada has people who try to make the world a better place to live.

Many famous Canadians are from Nova Scotia.

Canada has Sarah McLachlan, Abraham Gesner, Flora MacDonald, John Thompson, William Hall, and Rita MacNeil.

Canada has amazing people!

Nova Scotia Has Amazing People

Glossary
(All about what the words mean)

elected (page 12)
A person is elected when he or she has been chosen in a vote.

fuel (page 6)
Fuel is something that gives off energy when it is burned. Gasoline and coal are 2 kinds of fuel.

geologist (page 6)
A geologist is someone who studies rocks.

inventors (page 1)
An inventor is someone who creates something new.

justice (page 14)
A justice is a person who tries to decide who is right and who is wrong in court cases.

minister of foreign affairs (page 10)
The minister of foreign affairs takes care of Canada's friendships with other countries.

navy (page 20)
A navy is made of warships and the people who run them.

political party (page 10)
A political party is a group of people who agree on how Canada should be run. A political party tries to get its members elected to the government.

politicians (page 1)
Politicians are people who have been elected to government, or who are trying to be elected.

premier (page 14)
The premier is the leader of a province's government

prime minister (page 14)
The prime minister is the leader of Canada's government.

province (page 1)
A province is a separate region in Canada that has its own government.